The Fix-Its

Sally Odgers
Illustrated by Teresa Culkin-Lawrence

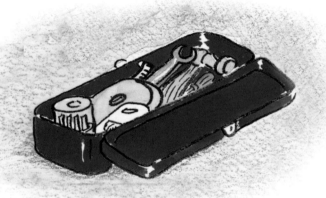

Contents

Chapter 1
A Clever Couple

Mr. and Mrs. Fix-It were clever at fixing things. If Mr. Fix-It found a broken toy, he would soon have it working again. Anything Mr. Fix-It fixed would be better than ever. Mrs. Fix-It was just as clever as her husband. She could fix all kinds of things, from teddy bears with missing ears to cupboard doors that wouldn't close.

The Fix-Its lived in a house that used to be run down. It took a lot of work for the Fix-Its to fix up the old house, but they enjoyed the job. They even built a workshop in the basement. Now the house looked as good as any house on the street!

People in the neighborhood noticed how clever the Fix-Its were and how cheerfully they worked.

Soon people began to call them whenever something needed fixing. The Fix-Its didn't mind. They would pack up some tools, jump in their little car, and drive off to fix whatever was broken.

"This is a great way to meet people," said Mrs. Fix-It.

Although the Fix-Its loved fixing things, sometimes they had problems.

"We can't pack all the things we need in our little car," said Mrs. Fix-It. "We have to leave some things at home. Then sometimes we find out we need them!"

"I know," said Mr. Fix-It. "I had to come home twice while I was fixing Mr. Cook's best chopping board. First, I didn't have my wood glue. Then, I had to get my clamp to hold the board steady while I fixed it!"

"It would be much easier if we had a van," said Mrs. Fix-It. "That way, we could carry all the tools we need for every job."

Mr. Fix-It grinned. "Maybe we could start our own fix-it business! We could buy a van and paint our name on it."

"We could have a website for advertising," said Mrs. Fix-It.

The Fix-Its got to work right away on their new fix-it business. They thought of a catchy slogan: LET THE FIX-ITS FIX IT!

The Fix-Its went to Mrs. Zeno's used car lot to choose a van for their new business. They found one inside the big showroom. It was large enough to hold all of their tools.

"There's just one problem," said Mrs. Zeno. "The showroom door is broken and I can't open it. You won't be able to have the van until I can get it fixed."

"We can fix it," said Mr. Fix-It, as he inspected the door. "This works on a pulley. The weight of the door must have caused the cable to break. We can replace the cable to fix the pulley. Then the door will open and close again."

Mrs. Zeno was delighted. "You should go into the fix-it business," she said.

"We plan to," said Mrs. Fix-It. "That's why we want the van. Look! We've even put our name on our overalls."

While Mr. Fix-It replaced the pulley, Mrs. Fix-It told Mrs. Zeno about their plans. Mrs. Zeno wished them the best of luck as they drove away.

Chapter 2
Happy to Help

Mr. and Mrs. Fix-It were about to start painting their new van when Mr. Ramos called.

"Oh Mr. Fix-It, my washing machine is spilling water all over my floor!" he cried. "Could you come and fix it?"

"Of course," said Mr. Fix-It. "We're happy to help!"

"Do we have the right tools?" said Mrs. Fix-It. "We'll need pliers to undo nuts and bolts."

"There might be loose screws, too," said Mr. Fix-It. "Let's take the screwdriver."

When the Fix-Its reached Mr. Ramos's house, he was mopping the floor. There was a terrible mess.

"I hope you can get the washing machine away from the wall," said Mr. Ramos. "It's very heavy."

"We can use a hand truck," said Mrs. Fix-It. "I'll just slip the flat metal part under the washing machine. Then I'll use the handle like a lever, and roll it away from the wall. I couldn't possibly lift this weight in my arms, but with a hand truck I can do it easily."

Mr. Fix-It looked inside the washing machine. "The screws have come loose," he said. "The bowl where you put the clothes should be held steady, but it has slipped to one side. We need to tighten the screws, and replace the rubber belt that drives the machine. Then everything will be fine."

Mr. Fix-It tightened the screws. Then he replaced the rubber belt. It was a kind of pulley that gripped the bowl and helped make it steady when the machine was turned on.

"All fixed!" he said.

Mrs. Fix-It wheeled the washing machine back where it belonged.

Mr. Ramos was delighted. "You should start your own fix-it business," he said.

"We're going to," said Mrs. Fix-It. She told Mr. Ramos all about their plans.

"You should paint your slogan and telephone number on your van," said Mr. Ramos. "Then everyone would know who you are and what you do."

"It's on the *to-do* list," said Mr. Fix-It. "We'll go home and do it now."

Chapter 3

Repairing and Preparing

By the time the Fix-Its reached home, it was too dark to paint their van. They decided to design their website instead.

Mr. Fix-It sat on the heavy chair in front of the computer. *Crack!* One of the legs broke.

"We'd better fix that," said Mr. Fix-It with a grin. "It wouldn't do for people who own a fix-it business to sit in a broken chair."

"You're right," laughed Mrs. Fix-It. "It wouldn't be a good advertisement!"

Mr. Fix-It fetched the toolbox and removed the screws that held the broken chair leg. Then he went down to the workshop to make a new leg that would match the others.

He screwed the new leg carefully into place.
"All fixed!" he said.

But by the time Mr. Fix-It had fixed the
chair, it was too late to design their website.

"Never mind. We can do that tomorrow after
we paint the van," said Mrs. Fix-It cheerfully.

The next morning, the Fix-Its were looking forward to painting the van. They were ready to begin, but the lid of the paint can was sticking.

"I can't get this lid off," said Mr. Fix-It. "It's stuck tight!"

Mrs. Fix-It picked up a screwdriver.

"I'll use this to open the lid," she said. "I'll just slide the tip under the rim of the lid, and then press down on the handle."

"Good idea!" said Mr. Fix-It. "The screwdriver is like a lever."

"But let's not use it to stir the paint," said Mrs. Fix-It. "Paint will spoil a good screwdriver. We need to take good care of all our tools."

Suddenly, Mr. Fix-It remembered something. "We forgot to call Mrs. Baker," he said. "We were going to ask her to make us a cake to celebrate our new business."

"I'll call her now," said Mrs. Fix-It.

Chapter 4
A Cake Break

Mrs. Fix-It was just about to pick up the phone when it rang. It was Mrs. Baker.

"Good morning, Mrs. Baker," said Mrs. Fix-It. "I was going to call you to ask if you could make us a cake today."

"Yes, I've been baking cakes all morning," replied Mrs. Baker. "You can pick one up right now. But could you please bring your tool kit? I need your help."

"Of course," said Mrs. Fix-It. "I'll be right there. I'll put my tool kit in our new van and drive over."

"I didn't know you had a van," replied Mrs. Baker.

"I'll tell you all about it when I get there," said Mrs. Fix-It. She hung up the phone.

"Mrs. Baker has a cake ready for us," she told Mr. Fix-It. "I'm going to get it now. She also wants me to fix something while I'm there, so I'll take my tool kit. We'll paint the van when I get back."

"I'm sure I can find something around here to fix while you're away," said Mr. Fix-It. "That dining table leg is looking wobbly."

Mrs. Fix-It drove the van to Mrs. Baker's house. Mrs. Baker's kitchen was very hot from baking cakes all morning.

"I like to let the fresh air in while I cook," said Mrs. Baker. "But the window keeps blowing closed. I tried to prop it open with a stick, but the stick fell over."

"Is that what you would like help with?" asked Mrs. Fix-It.

"Yes, please. Is it something you can fix?" asked Mrs. Baker.

"Sure I can fix it," said Mrs. Fix-It. "All you need is a very simple machine called a wedge."

"Where do I get one?" asked Mrs. Baker.

"There's a small one in the van," responded Mrs. Fix-It. "The van is full of tools for our new fix-it business."

"That's exciting!" said Mrs. Baker.

Mrs. Fix-It went to get the wedge. "Look, Mrs. Baker. It's just a piece of wood shaped like a slice of cake. You push the narrow edge under your window like this, and press it into place. Now, the window will stay open."

"That's so easy!" said Mrs. Baker.
"Thank you. By the way, have you designed a
website for your business?"

"Not yet," said Mrs. Fix-It. "We've been
too busy. We need to paint our van, too. But
every time we begin work, someone asks us to
fix something for them."

"Whoops!" said Mrs. Baker, apologetically.

"I didn't mean you! I was glad to come
and get a cake," Mrs. Fix-It laughed.

"You do such good work," said Mrs. Baker.
"You should advertise your business more,
the way I do."

She handed Mrs. Fix-It a balloon. Written on the balloon was MRS. BAKER'S CAKES.

"I know," said Mrs. Fix-It. "But we seem to have the time to fix everything except our new business."

As Mrs. Fix-It waved goodbye, Mrs. Baker smiled. The Fix-Its weren't the only people who knew how to fix things. Mrs. Baker picked up her telephone and made some phone calls.

Chapter 5
All Fixed!

When Mrs. Fix-It got back home, her husband was fixing a bicycle.

"The gears aren't working well," Mr. Fix-It explained. "That makes it hard to ride up hill. But I'll have it fixed in no time."

"We have a lot of other things to do," said Mrs. Fix-It. "There's the van to paint. And we can't forget about our website."

Mrs. Zeno stopped by while the Fix-Its were talking. "Hi, Mrs. Baker just called me," she said. "She knows I like designing websites. She asked if I could help you. You fixed my showroom door, so I'd be happy to help you design your website."

Mr. and Mrs. Fix-it smiled. "That would be wonderful!" they said.

25

Mrs. Fix-It led Mrs. Zeno to the computer. She told Mrs. Zeno what they wanted the website to say. She also made a long list of all the different fix-it jobs she and Mr. Fix-It could do. Mrs. Zeno got to work right away.

Mrs. Fix-It decided to get ready to paint the van. But when she walked outside, she saw Mr. Ramos. He was already painting the van! *Let the Fix-Its Fix It!* had been painted along the side. On the other side was the Fix-Its' phone number. He'd even left a space to write the website address.

"Wow! That looks wonderful!" exclaimed Mrs. Fix-It.

"Mrs. Baker told us that you were too busy fixing things for other people to get your business ready. So we all decided to help," said Mr. Ramos.

Mrs. Fix-It called Mr. Fix-It outside. He was very surprised. The Fix-Its hadn't realized that the people they helped had become their friends.

The van was almost finished when Mrs. Baker came up the road. She was carrying a bunch of balloons and another freshly baked cake.

"The people at the balloon shop made these for you!" said Mrs. Baker, smiling. "They have your name and phone number written on them."

"How lovely!" cried Mrs. Fix-It. "Thank you, Mrs. Baker!"

She tied the balloons to the porch, where they bobbed in the breeze.

They were all admiring the balloons and sharing cake when the phone rang.

"It's Mr. Jakin," said Mrs. Fix-It. "He has a problem with the trapdoor to his attic."

"Maybe it needs a wedge," said Mrs. Baker.

"Or a new pulley?" suggested Mrs. Zeno.

"Maybe," said Mr. Fix-It. "Whatever it is, I'm sure we'll be able to fix it!"

Wedges

In the story, Mr. and Mrs. Fix-It use different kinds of tools and machines to fix things. One of these is a wedge.

Mrs. Fix-It uses the wedge to keep a window open. She places it between the window-frame and the windowsill. The force of the wedge makes the window stay in place.

Some wedges have a sharp edge. This kind of wedge is used to cut and split things. A knife is a wedge used for cutting food.

An axe is a kind of wedge used for cutting wood.

Write an Advertisement

Think of a machine you want to advertise. Think about why people might want to have the machine.

- Copy the chart below.
- In the first column, list details about how the machine looks.
- In the second column, list the things the machine can do and how it can help people.
- Write an advertisement for the machine. Use your chart to help you.

Name of machine: _____

What it looks like:	Why it is useful:

Think About The Story

In *The Fix-Its*, Mr. and Mrs. Fix-It fix things for many people. Think about these questions.

- What problem does Mrs. Zeno have at her showroom? How do the Fix-Its solve her problem?

- What machine does Mrs. Fix-It use to move Mr. Ramos's washing machine? How does it work?

- What other machines did the Fix-Its use in the story? How are these machines useful?

To learn more about different kinds of machines, read the books below.

SUGGESTED READING
Windows on Literacy
Simple Machines
Wheels Around Us